FOULSHAM'S NEW POPULAR HANDBOOKS

THE FIFTY BEST
PARTY GAMES

AMUSEMENT FOR ALL

BY

ARTHUR ANNESLEY ROSS

AN EASY GUIDE TO INDOOR AND
OUTDOOR PARTY FUN

LONDON
W. FOULSHAM & CO. LTD.
NEW YORK . TORONTO . TOWN CAPE . SYDNEY

W. FOULSHAM & CO. LTD.
Yeovil Road, Slough, Berks, England.

ISBN 0 - 572 - 00170 - 3

PRINTED IN GREAT BRITAIN AT
THE CAMELOT PRESS LTD, SOUTHAMPTON

THE FIFTY BEST PARTY GAMES

A New Popular Handbook

CONTENTS

PREFACE

THE knowledge that this little book would supply a long-felt want is sufficient apology for its appearance. The writer has himself experienced that feeling of utter dullness at autumn and winter parties traceable to a lack of even an elementary knowledge of most of the well-known humorous and rollicking party games.

Children, of course, may generally be relied upon to make their own fun, but how much more enjoyable can the evening be made if the games played are organized by one of the grown-ups!

Music and laughter, games and forfeits, are the essentials to the success of a jolly gathering, and the writer hopes that the collection of the "Fifty Best Party Games" to be found in the pages of this little book will give a great amount of pleasure both to young and old attending the thousand and one parties that are arranged during the autumn and winter months.

Never hesitate to change a game. The more varied the games, the more keen will be the appreciation and delight of the children.

Most of the games will be found within the easy understanding of even the tiny tots. A few, however, require the co-operation of fairly intelligent children on the threshold of their teens, and those that fall within this category include "Thought-Reading," "Dumb-Acting Rhymes," "The Two Hats," "The Egyptian Oracle," "The Dwarf Witch," "The Judge," "Drawing-Room Photography," and "The Spirit Rests."

The writer has been bold enough to include four original games of his own construction—namely, "Air Ball," "Red Indians," "Bamboo Race," and "Obstacle Hoop Race."

THE FIFTY BEST PARTY GAMES

HUNT THE RING

THIS game causes great amusement among young children, and is also keenly enjoyed by grown-ups.

To play the game, pass a piece of string through a small curtain ring, join the end to form a circle, then let your little friends stand round, taking the string in their hands. At the word "Go!" they run the string through their hands. This, of course, constantly changes the position of the ring. One of the players must stand in the middle of the circle, and, at intervals, may touch any hand he thinks fit. Directly he touches a hand it must be lifted. Should the ring be there, the player hiding it must go into the centre of the circle, the other taking his place.

CAT AND MOUSE

In playing this game, first form a circle holding hands up to make an arch between each. One player, called the "Cat," goes round outside the circle and touches anyone he pleases. The one touched becomes a "Mouse," and must dart away in any direction he wishes in and out of the arches. The Cat follows in exactly the same track. Should the Cat go through a wrong arch he must pay a forfeit; but he still remains a Cat. Should he catch his Mouse, he becomes a Mouse himself, the one caught then becoming the Cat.

PICK AND CUP

This is an excellent game and must be played very fast. Form sides, equal numbers; sit down on the floor opposite each other, about two yards apart. The first player is a Pick, the next a Cup, the next a Pick, and so on alternately, but the first and last player must be a Pick. The Cups hold their hands together so as to form a cup. Place on the floor at the same end of each column an apple, button, marble, stone, orange, and a bean or any other trifling articles that may be at hand. The articles at the end of each column must be identical in number and kind. An umpire must be chosen who starts the race—for race it is. At the word "Go!" the end boy or girl of each column picks up one of the articles from the floor and places it in the Cup next to him. The next must pick it out of the Cup and place it in the next Cup, and so on, until the last player, who is a Pick, places it on the floor.

Directly the first player has picked up one article and placed it in a Cup, he or she must pick up another immediately and pass in the same way, until all the articles are set going. The Picks must work at lightning speed, else the other side will win. The side that first has all the articles on the floor at the opposite end of the column from which they started, wins.

AIR BALL

Here is a new and original game, and one in which the children of to-day will take keen delight. Accustomed, as they are, to playing net ball, and similar pastimes, Air Ball will be welcomed almost as an old friend. At a party, recently, where we introduced it, the children became so interested that Air Ball was in favour almost the whole evening. To play the game, first secure a good Air Ball. Having done this, pick sides—say, seven a side, but five will do very well. Place six chairs facing another six chairs in two rows with about a yard and a half between each column of chairs. Six of each side then sit on the chairs, these players being "forwards." At the back of the chairs on each side stands a boy who is named a "back."

When the game commences the ball is thrown into the centre of the "forwards," who must hit it with their hands towards the opposite "back." The duty of each "back" is to prevent the ball touching the ground on his side of the chairs. If it does, it counts a goal to the other side.

No "forward" is allowed to get off his seat. If he does, it is a foul; and the umpire (who should be appointed before the game begins) must give a "free hit" to the other side. This is done by throwing the ball in the air high enough for the "back" to hit; and if he can so hit the ball that it falls to the ground on the opposite side, it counts a goal. No "forward" must attempt to stop it when it is a "free hit," but the "back" may defend his goal.

Each game should continue for ten minutes. If the party is large enough, make up several teams; so that the winners of the first game play the next team, and so on. The unbeaten side becomes the winning team.

HUNT THE THIMBLE

A really good game for both young and old. To play it, send everyone out of the room except the person who is going to hide the thimble—a silver or, better still, a gilded one. Place it so that everyone may see it without moving anything. Then ask all to come in, and hunt for it.

If one should see it, he must *not* call out, "There it is!" but must pass on without saying a word, and sit down when he comes to a chair.

All this sounds very simple; but it is not so easy to find the thimble if it is hidden with a little thought.

You can have the piano playing if you please—

softly when no one is near the thimble, and loudly when close to its hiding-place. But the game is, perhaps, best played without any music. Those failing to find the thimble will pay a forfeit.

Thought-Reading, No. 1

This is a very simple, yet very ingenious pastime. You must take one person into your confidence. First, tell your audience that you will inform them of any number they may think of, if they will all intently fix their minds on the number chosen. The number should not be more than three figures. You then retire from the room while they choose a number. On entering again, you go round to various members of the audience, in each case placing one of your hands on either temple. You ask them to think more intently of the number. Then you come to your confederate. He keeps his mouth closed and simply presses his teeth together, when the vibration is conveyed to the temples. Suppose the number chosen is twenty-five: he clenches his teeth twice; then makes a pause, and again clenches his teeth five times. Should a nought be in the number, he moves his head slightly to one side. If carefully done it cannot go wrong. Should the number be one hundred, he makes one clench of the teeth; then pauses, and turns his head slightly to the right, back again, and then to the right again. This conveys the information that there are two noughts after the figure of one.

A point we must mention, which is very important, is this: when you have found out the number from your confederate, do not announce it, but go on to a few more people, telling them it is very difficult, and request them to concentrate a little more. Then suddenly say, "I have it! it is twenty-five"—or whatever the number may be.

Thought-Reading, No. 2

The company may here decide on an article in the room—for example, the poker. A confederate is required who must remain in the room, but the Thought-Reader must leave the room while the article is being chosen. When this has been done he re-enters. The confederate now calls out a number of articles. When he mentions the right article, the Thought-Reader must say, "Yes"; but to all others, "No." You must tell the audience that when the article chosen is mentioned they must all think intently of it. This is the way it is done: The article having been chosen, you (the Thought-Reader) are called into the room, and your confederate commences to mention articles to which you answer, "No." You have previously arranged that whenever he mentions an article containing glass, he will call out the right article after it. Supposing the poker be chosen: the confederate begins, "Is it the piano-stool, chair, cigar-case, carpet, tongs, door-handle, book, candlestick, china cup, etc."—to all of which you must say, "No." Then he mentions a photo-frame. You say, "No." Then he says, "The Poker." You say, "Yes," because *the photo-frame contains glass*.

You are sure to be asked to repeat it. Next time you keep to the same guide; only arranging that the *third* article after mentioning glass shall be the right one. If you have to give a further demonstration, make it the sixth article after glass. By so doing you will completely mystify them all.

The Spirit Rests

"The Spirit moveth." *Answer:* "Let it move."
"The Spirit passes." *Answer:* "Let it pass."
"The Spirit rests." *Answer:* "On . . . (*name*)."

In this game you must have a confederate. You

tell the audience that you will go out of the room, and that your confederate (Mr. X) will communicate to you, by thought, the name of any person in the room whom he may choose for the experiment. As you go out, someone is sure to speak. This is the key for both of you—the last person to speak before you go out of the room.

Your confederate then places his hand over the head of a person and calls out, "The Spirit moveth" in a loud voice, so that you can hear outside the room. To this you answer, "Let it move." He then goes to another person, holds his hand above their head and says, "The Spirit passes." You answer, "Let it pass." He now goes to the person who spoke last and repeats the same performance, crying, "The Spirit rests"; and you say, "On So-and-so," calling out the name of the person who last spoke on your leaving the room. You must then at once re-enter the room and ask if you are right. You are sure to be requested to do it again, when you retire directly someone has spoken and repeat the performance. It will be a complete success if done properly.

THE BLIND MAN'S STICK

First form a circle of your friends. Then let one be blindfolded and stood in the centre, with a stick in his hand. The circle must keep moving round. The one in the centre keeps the stick low, and with it touches one of the circle. The player touched at once takes hold of the stick, when the whole circle must stand still. The Blind Man now vocally imitates some animal or call, such as "Milko!" "Co-oals!" "Rags and Bones!" etc., and this must be at once copied by the player holding the stick. The Blind Man then guesses who it is. If successful, they change places.

MUSICAL CHAIRS

Any number may join in the game. Suppose twenty people are playing: you must have nineteen chairs placed side by side alternately back to front. The players then dance round the chairs to lively music, and to some extent must keep time with the music—that is, if it be slow, they must move slowly; if fast, they must quicken up and go round the chairs at a smart trot. When the music ceases (as it must at frequent intervals), each player attempts to sit down. As there are only nineteen chairs for twenty players, one is left standing. That person retires, one chair is taken away, and the music starts again. This continues until they are all out but one, who becomes the winner.

To make this a really great success, the person at the piano must enter into the spirit of the game. He should commence with a few slow chords, then break into a rollicking dance, and finally stop playing altogether. When ready again, he should strike two chords—stop—and so on, varying it each time. Do not forget to take away a chair whenever a player goes out.

THE BLIND MAN'S TREASURE HUNT

Children delight to play this game, which is not only exciting, but may be made the means by which small gifts are distributed. First send all the children out of the room. Then place a number of parcels (which you must make up beforehand) on a table in the centre. Now bring in one child blindfolded, lead her up to the table, and let her handle all the parcels. She may choose one only, which she takes away with her, having strict instructions not to open it until told to do so. The speculation as to what it contains causes great excitement. Of course, you must have enough parcels to go round and these should

be both large and small. In one put, say, a piece
of coal, in another a bean, in another a walnut,
and so on. Here and there you place in something
nice, such as a small box of sweets, a small bottle
of scent, a pencil, a brooch, or a ring.

When all have chosen a parcel (and by the by you
will note most of them select the larger and those
that they find are hard) you call them into the room,
and one by one you tell them to open their parcel.
Great fun will be caused when a large parcel is opened
and found to contain a small piece of coal, or a potato,
as the case may be!

Dumb-Acting Rhymes

For this game half of the children go out of the
room. Those inside choose a word which must be a
verb (*i.e.*, play, run, hit, dance, etc.). The children
now enter the room and are told a word which rhymes
with the word chosen. Thus, say the word taken is
"dance." They are told that a word has been selected
rhyming with "lance." The children must dumb-act
the word they think it is. They will most likely act
a horse prancing about, when they will be immediately
hissed, as the word is not "prance." But if they begin
to dance they are clapped; and the other side go out
of the room to take their turn.

Blind Man's Buff

This is a very old game, but a very popular one
with young children. One of the party is chosen to
be Blind-Man. Of course, he is blindfolded, and has
to catch the others. When someone is caught, the
player blindfolded feels the hair, face, etc., and tries
to guess who the child is. If correct, then the one
caught has to be blindfolded.

TURNING THE BOARD

Let all the party sit making a large circle. Each one must be given the name of an animal, such as lion, horse, bear, sheep, pig, rat, etc. One person goes into the middle of the circle (which must be large) and spins a board—a bread-board will do well—at the same time calling out the name of one of the animals. The child bearing that name must jump up and pick up the board before it stops spinning. Should this player fail to do so, a forfeit must be paid. When the game is finished the forfeits are redeemed as follows:

The one who turns the board must sit down and call one of the players to kneel in front of her, resting her face in her lap. She then holds over her head one of the forfeits and says: "Here's a pretty thing—a very pretty thing; what's to be done to the owner of this pretty thing?" The player questioned must pronounce the sentence. She may suggest anything she pleases, which the person to whom the forfeit belongs must do before the article is returned.

Suitable penalties are given in another part of the book (see p. 37).

TO BLOW OUT THE CANDLE

This is an exceptionally simple game, and one that provides endless amusement, not only for the young, but adults also. All you have to do is to place a lighted candle on a small table at the end of the room. You then invite someone to try and blow it out. You will get plenty of volunteers, but only one at a time may attempt the task. Conduct him to the table, blindfold him, and tell him to take four steps backwards, then four steps forwards and blow out the candle. This seems a very easy thing to do, but you will find very few able to accomplish it. The fun will be great.

BIRDS OF THE AIR

To make this game a success, a grown-up had better take command, as some appropriate patter must be used.

All competitors must face the speaker, with the right hand placed upon the left arm. Each time the speaker mentions the name of a bird, the right hand of all the players must be raised and fluttered in the air to imitate a bird; should *birds* in general be mentioned, both hands must be fluttered by all. When an animal or anything that cannot fly is mentioned, the right hand must remain on the left arm. Of course, the speaker tries to make the players go astray, as a forfeit must be paid by anyone doing the wrong thing. All being ready, he begins to tell them a story after this style:

"I had just turned out of bed and was on my way to the bathroom. It was a beautiful spring morning, and the *birds*" (here all hands should flutter) "were singing charmingly. I opened the window, and on the lawn was a lovely *thrush*, trying to pull a *worm* out of the ground. A *blackbird* darted out of a bush and made a rush, but neither of them obtained the *worm*. When I went out the air was full of song from all kinds of *birds;* and in the tree on my right a *squirrel* was leaping about."

Let us review this little speech:

"It was a beautiful spring morning, and the birds" (all hands must flutter in the air). . . . "On the lawn a thrush" (all the right hands must flutter). . . . "A blackbird" (right hands again flutter) . . . "obtained the *worm*" (right hands must again be resting on the left arms). . . . "Songs from all kinds of birds" (all hands again flutter). . . . "A squirrel" (right hands once more replaced on left arms).

It is obvious that the more frequently the speaker varies his allusions from animals to birds, and *vice versa*, the greater will be the number of forfeits he obtains.

ROUND THE WORLD

In this game all must be seated in a circle, excepting one player in the centre who is blindfolded. Then each child is given the name of a city or country which he is told to remember. The player in the centre now begins by calling out, "London to Edinburgh." This means that the two children who represent London and Edinburgh must jump up and change seats, the player in the centre endeavouring to catch them as they pass. If he is successful, the one captured is then blindfolded, and proceeds to call out some other change—such as "Liverpool to New York."

The game is often played with the child in the centre of the circle not blindfolded; and when she calls out, "London to Edinburgh," she endeavours to sit down in one of the vacant seats while they are changing. The player then left without a seat takes her place, as in the case of the blindfold player.

O'GRADY SAYS

This game causes endless fun, and results in a rich crop of forfeits. One of the players must take command and call himself "O'Grady." Everything O'Grady says must be obeyed or a forfeit given. It should be remembered that before any order is *obeyed* it must be prefaced by the words "O'Grady says." Line the children up, and then let O'Grady commence as follows:

"O'Grady says: Quick March!" and all the children must march around. "O'Grady says: Hands up!" All hands must be put up. "Hands down!" All hands must remain up, as O'Grady did not give the order. "O'Grady says: Salute!" "O'Grady says: Wag heads!" "O'Grady says: Stand on right leg!" "Stand on left leg!" and all remain on right leg until further command is given, as O'Grady did not call out the order. For every mistake a forfeit must be paid.

Hissing and Clapping

Let the players sit in a semicircle with a vacant chair between each, the same number leaving the room. Each child occupying a chair names a player outside the room. Then one child at a time enters, and has to sit down in the chair next to the player who she believes has chosen her. If she is right she is clapped, and retires to another part of the room; but if she is wrong she is hissed, and goes out of the room again, when another child is called into the room, and goes through the same performance, until all have chosen correctly. All the children sitting must try to persuade each child as she enters to sit on *their* vacant chair, say, in the following fashion: "Do come and sit on my chair, Amy, dear. This is the chair; you know it is I who want you."

Electric Shock

In this game one child must volunteer to leave the room, and remain outside till requested to return, when she is to touch an article agreed upon in her absence by all the other players. The object being chosen (say, the fender), the child is called in and at once commences her quest. Complete silence should be kept, excepting that one person must say "No" in a low tone of voice to everything the seeker touches that is not the object selected. When she places her hand on the fender (which she will in due time) everyone must shout "Yes!" as loudly as possible. This it is which will, in the exceptional quietness, give the "electric shock."

THE MASTER'S ORDER

Sitting round in a circle (which may comprise any number), one player must begin by saying to his neighbour: "The Master has sent me to you." "For what?" replies the one addressed. "To work with me and do as I." At the same time the speaker must begin to beat his knee with his right hand. The second player sets to work in the same way, at the same time turning to his neighbour and repeating the statement made to him, until the whole circle is working.

The second time round the same thing is said, only the left hand beats the left knee.

Third time round all right feet wag. Fourth time round all left legs wag. Fifth time round all heads must wag, so that in the end the whole circle is working. Of course, any lapsing must be paid for in forfeits.

THE TWO HATS

Having placed the children in a row, one child is selected and given two hats. He then walks along the row and presents one hat to any player he chooses. The moment the child receives the hat he must do everything *contrary* to that being done by the owner of the other hat. If this player should put the hat on his head, his victim must keep *his* off. If he holds it in his left hand, the victim holds it in his right. Should he sit down, the victim must stand up—and so on. If the first player finds that no mistakes are being made (and therefore no forfeits forthcoming), he goes on to another, and tries different tactics. Forfeits are sure to result if smart things are done.

THE SUGAR HAT

This is an amusing trick that any child may perform with ease. The performer must first place a number of hats on a table and then ask for the sugar-basin. He next selects a lump of sugar, and says that he will swallow it, and, by a magical power which he possesses, will guarantee that it shall be under one of the hats—whichever the company may select. Of course, they all think he will secure another piece of sugar and endeavour to place it under the hat chosen, and therefore a very sharp lookout is kept on the sugar-basin. He swallows the sugar, asks which hat it is to be under, and on being told, places this on his own head—and, of course, fulfils the contract!

Finding the Halfpenny

The children here all sit round a table, keeping their hands well under it, excepting one of the players who is the "finder." A halfpenny is given them, which they must pass one to another. Should the halfpenny be passed to the child next to the "finder," this player must at once pass it back again. Directly the "finder" says, "Hands up!" all hands must be placed on the table, closed. He then points to a hand, which must at once be opened. Should the halfpenny not be there, the hands are again placed under the table, and round goes the halfpenny again, until he says, "Hands up!" If he guesses rightly, the one who had the halfpenny becomes the "finder."

Avoid-the-Hassock Dance

Here is a game that will afford endless amusement to players and spectators alike. Place a hassock on end in the middle of the room, and form a circle about it. Begin by dancing around. Then one player must try to draw the other on to the hassock, so as to knock it over. Should anyone touch it and cause it to fall over, he must retire; and the others continue until two only are left in, in which case the conqueror wins. The fun is great, and often when you have one of the circle right against the hassock, he will jump over and back again in his endeavour to avoid knocking it over.

HUNT THE SLIPPER

This, perhaps, is the oldest game on record; yet it is always popular. The children sit on the floor in a circle, with their toes touching. Then a person outside the circle brings a slipper to be mended (a small one), and leaves it. Returning in a few moments, she asks for the slipper, but it is not finished. She thereupon goes away, and returns later, and again asks for the slipper she left some days ago. They answer that the slipper is not finished yet; but she demands it, as she cannot wait any longer. The slipper cannot be found! *Then commences the hunt.* It is passed from one to the other, until the owner secures it.

THE EGYPTIAN ORACLE

This wonderful square has been handed down from the old Egyptians. To trace it back to its original source would be a task well-nigh impossible. The marvel of it is that it really seems to answer questions. The square, formed of letters, should be copied on a large piece of cardboard, and hung up in a room dimly lighted. If possible, let the person who works the Oracle be in Egyptian dress and carry a wand. He commences by asking if there is anyone present who would like to consult the Egyptian Oracle, which answers any question. As everyone will want to do so, they must be dealt with one at a time.

The Oracle must first ask for the question. Having obtained it, he writes it down on a piece of paper and hands it to the one who is asking the question. He next requests him to come up to the square and choose a letter. The questioner may select any letter on the square. The Oracle then hands him the pencil and asks him to put down the following letters as called out. We will presume that the question asked is: "Shall I retire from business?" The letter chosen is *s*. The Oracle then places his wand on the letter *s*, second column, fourth line, and calls out, "S." He next takes every fifth letter from there, reading from left to right until he comes round again to the letter from whence he started. Always remember the first letter come to on the top line, as the answer will begin at that letter. Having begun with *s*, the next letter will be *i*, next *t*, next *w*, next *i*, next *l*, next *l*, next *d*, next *o*, next *w*, next *r*, next *o*, next *n*, next *g*, next *w*, next *h*, next *o*, next *d*, next *o*, and finally *e*. Taking them in order, they read "sitwilldowrongwhodoe." This does not make sense until you know the key. As the first letter reached on the top line of the square was the third *w*, you start with that letter, which makes it read, "Who does it will do wrong."

The greater the air of mystery you throw around it, the more you will impress your audience. This Oracle can be used with great success at bazaars, etc.

d	w	w	a	w	o	h	a	b	h
i	o	i	s	o	t	d	t	t	w
w	o	a	a	a	i	e	n	i	i
t	s	d	n	t	h	i	a	a	e
o	t	t	n	t	u	w	t	d	h
t	i	a	e	s	f	l	i	n	u
e	l	n	j	c	a	d	t	o	c
r	o	h	y	e	o	w	y	p	e
f	r	w	e	d	i	o	i	a	e
l	n	s	c	t	l	g	h	e	h

KEEP THE FEATHER FLYING

To play this game a small circle must first be formed, all sitting close together. Then take a fluffy chicken's feather and cut off the stem. The game commences by someone letting go the feather above the heads of the children in the circle. The object of each is to prevent the feather touching them. If it touches any player, that one must pay a forfeit. Therefore, directly the feather comes near a player he endeavours to blow it away to another child, and so the excitement increases. Remember the feather must be very light.

THE WITCH'S ORACLE

This Oracle will cause both fun and astonishment. It consists of six sets of figures by which, if you carefully follow the instructions, you will be able to tell the age of anyone up to sixty, or any number of which one of the company may think. Children do not mind their ages being known, but in the case of a lady above thirty, it is, perhaps, best to request that they think of a number under sixty. The success of this kind of amusement is always the more fully assured if the one who works the Oracle is dressed as a witch and carries a wand. We here give the six sets of figures, which must be copied on to large pieces of cardboard and hung up in a prominent position.

You tell the audience that by a wonderful gift you are able to inform them all what age they were last birthday. The children are certain to come forward.

You take the first Child up to Card No. 1, and ask her if her age is set down there. If it is, she must answer, "Yes"; and if it is not, she is to say, "No." You take her to each card in order, and remember to which card she replies "Yes." You then add up the right-hand upper corner figures, which will give you her age correctly.

Let us take an example. Say the first child's age is twelve. We look through Card No. 1, and find that it does not contain the number 12. Then we go to card No. 2, and here we find it mentioned; therefore, we remember Card 2. We next take card No. 3, and find it is not there. Passing on to Card 4, we find it there, and remember Card 4. In Card 5 it is not; and the last card, No. 6, also does not contain it. We have therefore only two cards in this case—Nos. 2 and 4. Now take the right-hand upper corner

1.

3	5	7	9	11	1
13	15	17	19	21	23
25	27	29	31	33	35
37	39	41	43	45	47
49	51	53	55	57	59

2.

9	10	11	12	13	8
14	15	24	25	26	27
28	29	30	31	40	41
42	43	44	45	46	47
56	57	58	59	60	13

3.

17	18	19	20	21	16
22	23	24	25	26	27
28	29	30	31	48	49
50	51	52	53	54	55
56	57	58	59	30	60

4.

5	6	7	13	12	4
14	15	20	21	22	23
28	29	30	31	36	37
52	38	39	44	45	46
47	53	54	55	60	13

5.

3	6	7	10	11	2
14	15	18	19	22	23
27	27	30	31	34	35
38	39	42	43	46	47
50	51	54	55	58	59

6.

33	34	35	36	37	32
38	39	40	41	42	43
44	45	46	47	48	49
50	51	52	53	54	55
56	57	58	59	60	41

figure of each, and add together—that is, 8 and 4, which makes 12. This is the age of the child we took as an example.

THE DWARF WITCH

Here we have something which, if trouble be taken to prepare properly, will not only create laughter and bewilderment among the little ones, but will also mystify the grown-ups. Some time back we saw this trick performed at a party, the whole audience being amazed. Perhaps it would be well to relate it just as we witnessed it on that occasion.

The scene was a dining-room with a bay window, across which was drawn heavy curtains, meeting in the middle. A small table was placed where the curtains met, the legs of the table being hidden by baize, which was pinned around. Two people performed this trick. One had his face made up like an old witch with long grey hair and a witch's hat. The same person had placed a pair of socks on his hands so that the upper part extended well over the wrists, and his hands into slippers. A dark red pinafore was pinned round to look like a skirt and bodice. He stood behind the table where the curtains met, putting his slippered hands on the table. The curtains were pinned just behind his head, and directly under the table, so that all the audience could see was the head down to the hands, which were resting on the table to represent feet. Now the witch was complete, all but the arms and hands. The other person, standing behind, then pushed his arms through the armholes of the pinafore, but only just far enough to appear in keeping with the size of the witch—just sufficient to enable the hands to reach the witch's face. A pair of long mittens were next placed on the wrists. We then had a perfect dwarf. The voice was disguised, and the hands moved in harmony with what was being said. Now and then the hand was raised, to scratch the head or face; and when the witch coughed, the hand was raised to the mouth. Fortunes were told, people coming right up to the dwarf and placing their hands in hers without detecting the trick. While the witch was telling the fortune a finger of one of the hands was pointing to the lines in the person's hand. The two actors used their imagination, and the old witch chuckled, laughed, and danced with her slippered hands, to the delight of all.

It is well to have a stage-manager, who might announce early in the evening that the hostess had engaged the famous witch "Zaza," measuring only two feet in height, and whose age was a hundred and fifty-six, to tell the fortune of anyone in the room. This will give rise to much speculation and wonderment, and all will be looking forward to the time when she will appear.

When this time arrives, set chairs for the grown-ups and a few for the children. The manager should then make an appropriate speech, and at its conclusion say, "Now I will introduce to you the wonder of the age—the renowned witch 'Zaza' "—at the same time drawing back a little curtain, which you must fix over the witch previously. Of course, there will be much clapping of hands and roars of laughter, during which the witch must bow, chuckle, and dance. Our advice is to have one or two rehearsals, when success will be certain.

THE JUDGE

To get the most fun out of this game, it is well for boys to choose girls as partners; but if this is not possible, they can take boys. Form as many couples as you please, and let them all sit in a row, with a space between each couple, so that the Judge can easily know who should answer his questions. When all is ready the Judge must walk, with a stately air, up and down the row of couples—assuming a very grave face and bearing. He may stop at any couple, and speak to one of them. Should he address a boy, he (the boy) must not answer, but his partner (girl or boy, as the case may be) must reply. Should the person addressed answer, forfeit is demanded. This game causes great merriment. Let us give an example:

The Judge stops before a boy and girl couple, and says, in a most stately voice, "Sir, you are a fine specimen of manhood, with a clear eye and intelligent face. Tell me what profession in life you would like to take up." The boy must not say a word, but the girl answers, "If you please, sir, dressing dolls." Then, of course, when a girl is addressed, her partner, if it be a boy, says something equally unsuitable. A good deal depends on the Judge. If he is clever, and makes suitable speeches to each couple, the game will be a great success.

THE SIXPENCE THAT STICKS

This is a simple little trick, but one that causes a great deal of merriment among the children. You tell the audience that you will stick a sixpenny-piece on a boy's forehead by wetting it with plain water, so that he will not be able to shake it off. He must not use his hands; but can put his head at any angle and shake as much as he pleases. The way to proceed is this: Take a sixpence and wet it with water. (This is not really necessary, but you have said you would use water.) Then lay the sixpence on the boy's forehead, and press it down fairly hard for a short period, saying that it takes a little time to stick. In less than a minute you can remove your hand, but you must be careful to take the sixpence away with it and without the boy's knowledge. This is easily done if you slide your hand upwards towards the top of his head. Although the sixpence is not there, the boy will think it is, for it will feel to him as if it were. He will shake and turn his head, but to no purpose; until he gives it up, and puts his hand to his forehead to pick the sixpence off. His surprise at not finding it there will be great. The fun is increased by the remarks of the boys, which usually take this form: "Shake it off, Jack. Don't be done. Anyone could do it; a baby could get that off in a tick." This trick invariably amuses the grown-ups as much as the children.

ROUND THE POKER

This is a game that causes much merriment, and is very popular with the boys. Place a table at the end of the room, and a cigar-box on the table, end up. On the top of this deposit a chocolate. Then take the first boy, who must be about four yards away from the table, and tell him to put his forehead on the knob of a poker which you have placed before him. (The poker must be touching the floor.) Then tell him to turn round four or five times, let go the poker quickly, walk straight to the table, and pick the chocolate off the cigar-box. He must go straight there; if he stops he is disqualified. Should he knock the chocolate down, it does not count. He must pick it up cleanly with his fingers. You will find few able to do this. Some will stumble in quite a different direction; some will hardly be able to move at all. If a player succeeds in picking up the chocolate, it becomes his.

BALANCING THE BOTTLE

This trick is difficult, though every now and then you will find a boy who is able to do it. But the fun is great, whether it is accomplished or not. This is how it is done:

Almost fill a champagne bottle with water—about three-quarters full. Place a sixpenny-piece on the floor on a piece of paper so that it can be clearly seen, then poise the bottle very nearly on the back of your head. The object is to get down, pick up the sixpence with your lips, and again rise without upsetting the bottle. It sounds as if this could not well be done, and that a bottle or two would be broken; but that is not so. If the bottle topples over, the hand will naturally fly up and catch it; should it fall to the ground it will not break. The bottle now being well back on the crown of your head, bend forward, so that when you reach the ground the bottle will be in an upright position. The sixpence should be a little more than your own length away from you when you start. Having settled the bottle comfortably on your head, you begin to bend your knees carefully, until you can reach the floor with one hand. Then get the other hand on the floor, to steady yourself. Now creep forward on your hands, until you can free your legs, which will bring you into a flat position on the ground. Then begin to draw yourself up to the sixpence with your hands. Once you are there, you will find no difficulty in getting hold of the sixpence with your lips. To do this, place them round the coin with your teeth closed, and suck in your breath. You will,

as the result, find the coin come up into your mouth.
Having got so far, you must be just as careful going
back. Raise yourself on your hands, and gradually
get into the same positions as you were in getting
down—knees bent, hands touching the ground, etc.
Now be careful, for it is so easy to spoil it all by inatten-
tion. If it is thought inadvisable to use a coin, a handkerchief might well be substituted.

THE BIRD-SNATCHER

For this game you need your audience in a close
circle. One of the party must be the "Snatcher";
and it is best to choose him from the older ones, as a
good deal depends on the story that he tells.

All the children in the circle take the name of a
bird. This they must remember. The only name
that may not be used is the Bat. All hands must be
placed on knees. Should the "Snatcher" mention,
say, a Blackbird, the child who has that name must at
once place his right hand behind his back. If the
"Snatcher" names a Bat, all hands must go behind
the back, and must remain there until another bird is
mentioned. The object of the "Snatcher" is to capture
a hand during the moving of hands. If he does so,
the one caught has to pay a forfeit, and becomes the
"Snatcher."

The "Snatcher" begins in this fashion:

"The other day, as I was walking down a lane, the
whole countryside seemed to be alive. Animals darted
here and there, and birds sang loud and sweetly. I
came to a very tall tree, and there was a beautiful
Thrush." (Here the "Snatcher" makes a dive for the
Thrush's hand; but failing to secure it, he goes on.)
"In the hedge was a Robin." (Again a dive for the
hand, which he misses; and thinking it time for a
change, continues.) "But in an old, decayed oak-tree
I saw a large Bat." All hands attempt to fly behind

backs; but he captures one. A forfeit is demanded, and this person has then to become the "Snatcher."

Every child failing to put both hands behind his back when the Bat is mentioned must pay a forfeit.

CHARADES

We cannot say with authority when the charade was first played; it is, however, without doubt, one of our oldest games, and always popular. Children love charades, and at a party generally wish to know when they are to be played.

By way of preparation a few shawls, hats, and jackets will suffice. If some false hair is available, so much the better. It is best to select the children for the principal parts, as special intelligence is here needed. The word chosen for the charade must be of two syllables. We give here a few words that are suitable: Willow, milkmaid, hardship, earshot, mistake, madcap, childhood, grandfather, grandchild, namesake, waistcoat, joyful, full-blown, handsome, quicksand, nutmeg, quicktime, roundhead, tearful, tunnel, tartar, outside, inside, homesick, armchair, bonfire, daybreak, surname, perform, intent, leap-year, footman, wayward, tintack, lifelong, lifelike, cutlet, cupboard, starting, thoughtful, damage, watchman, encase, indent, inform, moonstruck, indoor, outdoor. Now for an example:

Say we take the word "Milkmaid." The first scene must then introduce the word "Milk." The stage setting should be a drawing-room with a lady sitting on a settee.

Characters.

Lady of the House	...	MRS. FLAIRUP.
Maid ...	... ...	JACKSON.
Visitor	... ...	MRS. KNOWALL.

Enter JACKSON.

Jackson: Mrs. Knowall has called, madam.

Mrs. Flairup (rising): How do you do, Mrs. Knowall? I am so glad to see you. (Says aside to Jackson) Bring in tea.

Mrs. Flairup: Come and sit down, and we will have a cosy little chat before tea.

(They talk ordinary conversation.)

Enter Jackson with tea. She upsets milk.

Mrs. Flairup: How dare you be so careless, Jackson! You have stained my dress.

Jackson: It was an accident, madam.

Mrs. Flairup: That will do, Jackson.

Mrs. Knowall: Milk stains so. I should sponge it with very hot water.

Mrs. Flairup: Yes, I think I must. It is so annoying to spoil a new dress in these terrible times; but I am afraid I spoke a little too severely to Jackson. I was so annoyed.

Mrs. Knowall (rising): I think I must be going. It has been such a pleasure seeing you again. I hope you will pay me a visit before long.

Mrs. Flairup, also rising, rings the bell; and Mrs. Knowall departs.

End of First Scene.

Second Scene.

Characters.
Lady of the House   ...   Mrs. Flairup.
Maid ...   .   Jackson.
(In this scene we must introduce the word "Maid." Setting same as last—a drawing-room. Mrs. Flairup reading book.)

Enter Jackson.

JACKSON: If you please, madam, I have come to give you notice; and I wish to leave as soon as possible.

MRS. FLAIRUP: Why, Jackson, what is all this about? I thought you were very comfortable here, and would stay with me for quite a long time.

JACKSON: Yes, madam, I am very comfortable here; and I was happy up to yesterday. But I have never before, in all the places I have had (which I must say are not many, as I always kept my situations), been "told off" as I was yesterday—and in front of visitors, too. I was never so insulted in my life.

MRS. FLAIRUP: Now, Jackson, calm yourself, and remember to whom you are talking. You know I was very much annoyed. I wore that new dress yesterday for the first time, and to be so spoilt—well, it would annoy anyone.

JACKSON: I grant all that, madam, but I have never been "told off" before in front of visitors.

MRS. FLAIRUP: Well, Jackson, forget it. I am sure we suit each other very well, and you know I should have great difficulty in getting another maid—they are so scarce. I will consider raising your wages at the end of the month.

JACKSON: Very well, madam; if you put it that way, I withdraw my notice.

[*Exit* JACKSON.

End of Second Scene.

THIRD SCENE.

Characters.

MRS. SNOWBALL ... *Who keeps a dairy.*
JACKSON ... ... *Mrs. Flairup's Maid.*
(*Here we have to introduce the whole word—"Milkmaid."
Setting a dairy, with woman—*MRS. SNOWBALL—*behind counter.*)

JACKSON: Good-morning, Mrs. Snowball; a beautiful morning.

Enter JACKSON.

MRS. SNOWBALL: Yes, you're right, it is; but what brings you out so early?

JACKSON: Well, I had a bit of a tiff with the missus yesterday, and I told her off, and gave her notice. But, of course, she didn't want me to go, as I am a good servant, and knows my job from A to Z. So she asked me to stay on with a rise in wages. I says, Yes, I would. This morning she says, "Jackson, would you like to go for a walk? You look pale, as if you want some air." So I says, "Yes, madam." And she says, "Well, will you run along and pay Mrs. Snowball's bill? It is overdue." So here I am to pay your bill.

MRS. SNOWBALL: I think you did right in staying. Although there are plenty of places going, there are very few decent ones, and your lady is a good sort.

JACKSON: You're not looking very grand, Mrs. Snowball.

MRS. SNOWBALL: Oh, I am all right; only a little worried. One of our milkmaids has gone and poisoned her finger, and I can't for the life of me get another. I don't know what we shall do.

JACKSON: Well, worry doesn't make it any better. You are sure to find someone to help you for a short time, until she is better. Well, I must be going. Good-bye, Mrs. Snowball.

MRS. SNOWBALL: Good-bye.

End of Charade.

The audience will most likely guess the word, as it is a fairly easy one. But this charade is not at all difficult to play.

Drawing-Room Photography

One person must go out of the room, having a confederate, who remains. He, the confederate, must make a little speech on photography, and say that he is prepared to take a photograph of anyone in the room, although it will not be visible to those in the room. The Master, who is out of the room, will readily recognize who it is.

He then secures a piece of paper, or a piece of music, and asks who would like to have their photo taken. When one has been chosen, he tells her to pose herself and look happy. He next proceeds to sensitize the piece of music, or paper, by rubbing it. He then holds it in front of the child who is to be photographed, telling her to keep quite still and look pleasant. After a moment or so he says it is taken, and must now develop it. This he does by holding it to the fire, lamp or gas, for a few moments. He then says it is a fine photo, and the Master is asked to come in.

On entering the room, the photo is handed to the Master, while his confederate (who has retired to a seat), at once assumes the attitude of the child he has taken—such as legs crossed, hands folded in lap, head on one side. The Master notices his attitude, looks for a child sitting in that position, and, of course, at once recognizes who it is. He then says, "What a capital photograph! There can be no doubt as to who it is"; and finally mentions the name.

Although this is all very simple, it will give rise to a deal of wondering as to how it is done; and you will surely be asked to do it again.

Forfeits

1. Place a poker on the ground so that you cannot jump over it. (It should rest against the wall.)

2. Bite an inch off the poker. (Hold the poker an inch from your mouth, and bite.)

3. Play a tune on the piano.

4. Sing a verse of a song.

5. Recite.

6. Put your right hand where your left cannot touch it. (Place it on the left elbow.)

7. Kiss the girl or boy you like best in the room.

8. Sing in one corner, cry in another, laugh in another, and dance in another.

9. Dance a jig.

10. Kiss your shadow.

11. Kiss a book inside and out, without opening it. (Kiss a book inside the room, and then take it outside and kiss it.)

12. Place two chairs together. Take off your shoes and jump over them. (You put two chairs together. Take off your shoes and jump over the shoes.)

13. Place a candle so that everyone in the room can see it, but you yourself cannot. (On your head.)

14. Say the alphabet backwards.

15. Hop round the room on one leg.

16. Repeat five times quickly, "The Horn of the Hunter was Heard on the Hill."

17. Touch thousands at the same time. (Place your hand on your head.)

18. Kiss yourself in the looking-glass.

19. Spell "Constantinople" backwards.

20. Put yourself through a keyhole. (Write "yourself" on a piece of paper and pass it through the keyhole.)

21. Jump over the moon. (Draw the moon on a piece of paper and jump over it.)

22. Kiss your hostess's hand.

23. Lie down on the floor, fold your arms, and get up again without unfolding them.

24. Sit upon the fire. (Write the words "the fire" on a paper, and sit on it.)

25. Leave the room with two legs and return with six. (Walk out of the room and return with a chair.)

GARDEN GAMES

GAMES FOR A TEENAGE PARTY

GARDEN GAMES

Potato Race

This is one of the most popular of outdoor games. It may be played by children or adults—on a lawn, or any ground where freedom of movement is possible.

Commence by placing in line five plates, about a yard and a half in front of each other. In each plate set a teaspoon. Walk to the right or left—say, fifteen yards—and place five more plates exactly opposite the others, with five potatoes on each. Let the potatoes be of different sizes, but none very small.

Five players now line up by the five plates with spoons on them, and at the word "Go!" they must each pick up the spoon in the plate belonging to them, race to the plate opposite, scoop up a potato, and race back again, depositing the potato in the empty plate. Should a potato be dropped on the way, the player must go back, scoop it off the ground, and race on again as fast as possible. This must continue until each player has transferred the five potatoes to the plate from which they started. The right hand only must be used.

If there are a number of players, divide them up into teams, the first two of each heat to race in the final.

Red Indians

This game is more suitable for boys than girls, although the latter join in with equal delight. If, however, you can secure two teams of boys, a far better result is assured.

One side is generally called Red Indians, and the other British.

The game is played as follows:

The British select a camp—the best place is an open space in a shrubbery. Guards are put out at different points to give the alarm should the enemy attack. The camp is supposed to be in danger from Red Indians.

The Red Indians choose a camp, unknown to the British, and send out scouts to discover the strength of the British, and where their guards are placed. When one of the guards is located, the scouts retire to their camp and plan to take him prisoner. The object of the Red Indians is to capture the British flag. Of course, each side selects a Commander-in-Chief, and he chooses his captains, etc. If the Chief acts intelligently, he will lead his men to victory.

The Indian Chief commences by sending a scout out to find the whereabouts of the British outposts. When the scout has ascertained this, he reports to his Chief, who at once sends a few men to capture one of these outposts. With his main force the Chief makes off to another point. When the attack is made on the British outpost, the Indians purposely create a great noise, and try to drag the guard away. He, of course, will cry out for assistance; and it is more than likely that the *whole* of the British will rush to his rescue. Then the Red Indians, with a tremendous war-cry, swoop down on the camp and endeavour to capture the flag.

We have given an outline only of the game, for it is our experience that the boys invariably form plans of their own.

GARDEN ROUNDERS

The game of Rounders is a very old English one, of which the national game of America (baseball) is no doubt a variation. The correct number to play the game is eighteen—nine on each side; but this is not arbitrary, as five or six a side will suffice. Should you be playing five a side, it is policy to do away with one of the bases.

We here give a diagram, showing how the bases should be arranged.

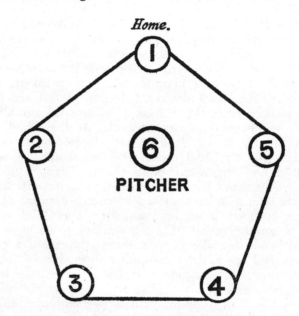

Position No. 1 is Home, and where the hitter stands. No. 6 is where the bowler or pitcher stands. A tennis-ball is the most suitable for garden play, and a cut-down broom-handle will do for a bat. The pitcher must send full pitches to the hitter, who has a right to refuse any ball he does not fancy, the number generally being arranged beforehand. For instance, say that four balls are agreed upon. He can refuse three; but the next is his last chance, and he must run whether he hits it or not. If he misses it, the fielder standing behind him (acting wicket-keeper, as in cricket) catches the ball if he can, and places it on base No. 1 before the hitter has time to reach base No. 2. This makes him out. The ball is not in play until it has been struck. When it is in play, and one of the fielders throws the ball up so that it hits one of the side batting whilst the latter is between any of the bases, that person is out. If a ball is caught, the whole side is out.

The last man in has the choice of three balls; but he cannot make use of any bases. He must, on hitting the ball, go right round—that is, from Home through bases 2, 3, 4, 5, back to Home. Should one of the fielders send the ball in to the keeper to place it in Home before the hitter arrives there, or should the latter be hit by the ball whilst running, the whole side is out. On the other hand, should he reach Home before the ball and without being hit, it counts a rounder, and puts the whole side in again.

Any player, having hit the ball, can run to base No. 1, and if he thinks it safe, on to No. 2 or 3, or right round; but if he stops at any base, he must not start again until the ball is in play. No two players can stay at one base. The striker, having hit the ball and started to run, must drop the bat. The pitcher has the right to arrange the field as he pleases. Supposing the game has commenced, and a ball hit. The striker runs through base No. 2 and stops at No. 3. Another takes the bat, and hits the ball. The player at No. 3 can run on through Nos. 4 and 5, and back Home. In this case he is not out, but it does not score. To score, you must make a complete round without stopping at any base.

A rounder can be scored in any part of the game, but the last man in must score a round, or the whole side is out.

The side who score the most rounders win.

SACK RACE

Boys keenly enjoy this race, which is also very entertaining to the spectators. Having obtained, say, half a dozen sacks, the boys racing are instructed to get into them, when the sacks are tied loosely round their necks. The boys are next lined up, and at the word "Go!" are started on their thirty yards' race. There will no doubt be many tumbles, but those who fall must rise again and continue the race.

The styles of progression are varied and peculiar: some will jump along, while others will take a short run or shuffle. The competitor who comes in first will, of course, win the race.

TUG-OF-WAR

This game can be played by girls and boys, separately or together. First, make sides: the number does not matter, so that it be the same on either side. Draw a line and place a rope across. Each side then takes hold of the rope (leaving about two yards clear either side of the line) and endeavours to pull the other just over. Whichever side is successful in two out of three trials, wins.

THREE-LEGGED RACE

This race is so well known that very little explanation is necessary. However, first tie the left leg of one boy to the right leg of another (round their ankles), and then, when you have all the couples ready, start them off for, say, a fifty yards' race.

If those competing can obtain a little practice with their partners beforehand, it will be possible to produce quite a respectable pace.

TORTOISE RACE

This is necessarily a slow race, and over a very short course—about ten yards. Contrary to all other races, it is the *last* in who wins.

Start the competitors off in a line, and tell them they must keep moving—but as slowly as they please. Anyone who stops is disqualified. There should be two or three umpires watching, and should these detect any racer stopping, even for a second, the defaulter should at once be disqualified.

SKIPPING

Although this pastime does not require any explanation (every boy and girl being able to skip), we suggest that it is well to have a skipping-rope or two at every party. Girls in particular delight in the exercise, and many an exciting competition can be arranged.

JUMPING

This, again, requires little or no explanation. It will, however, amuse both boys and girls. Divide the time at your disposal between a long jump and then a high jump.

BAMBOO RACE

This is an original game requiring some skill; and it will be found very popular. You first secure a few bamboo poles, about six feet long—the longer the better. Each racer places one of these horizontally on his, or her, head. It is best for two to race at a time and the course to be in the shape of a square. Any child can balance a bamboo on his, or her, head, and go at a good pace on the straight; but the fun commences when the first corner is reached, for unless great care be exercised in turning, the bamboo will certainly fall off. With a little skilful manoeuvring the course can be successfully negotiated.

BOUNCING BALL

In this game a large gutta-percha ball is required. Having placed the children in a circle—about two yards between each—throw the ball into the middle of them. One child then rushes out and bounces the ball on its rebound, with the palm of the hand, *once only*. The child next to her then does likewise, and so the game goes on right round the circle. Any player bouncing the ball *twice* drops out, and the game continues until there is one only left in, who becomes the winner.

AIR BALL

For this game you want a strong air balloon, slightly heavier than the ordinary kind. Place two sticks on the ground, about four yards apart, horizontally. Then opposite them, twenty yards away, two more sticks. These are the goals. There should be seven players on each side, but five will do. Choose one for goal-keeper, one for right wing, and one for left wing. The rest are forwards.

The opposing sides line up in the centre, facing each other, with about one yard between each line. The ball is then thrown into the air. Each side must endeavour (by hitting the ball only when it is in the air) to place it between the two posts opposite them. If successful, this counts a goal. Should the ball touch the ground, the umpire must again throw it into the air, and at the place where it fell.

CROSS TOUCH

This is an excellent game for the garden. Any number can take part; it must be played "fast and furious." One boy is selected as Touch. It is then his business to name another boy, whom he at once chases and endeavours to touch; but should any other boy pass between them, he then has to rush after that player; and again, if anyone else crosses between them, he must at once run after that particular one; and so on, until he touches a player who has not been crossed, who at once changes places with him, and in his turn becomes Touch.

FOLLOW MY LEADER

Any number can take part in this game, which requires a leader, preferably a player with some imagination.

First line all up in a long row, each behind the other, with two yards between them, the leader being about ten yards ahead. Whatever the leader does, all must do. Should anyone fail, he must retire to the end of the row, but still continue in the game. The object is to be head of the row.

Now, the leader may do a thousand different things, which all must copy; but he should never attempt anything dangerous. We have seen this game played by boys all of about the same age (ten to twelve years) with a daring leader, who, in his progress, caught the branch of a tree, pulled himself up and over the other side, and then rushed off, and leapt over a ditch filled with water. Of course, some failed and had to go back to the end of the row. Let the leader do anything he chooses—the greater the variety the better; but he should avoid foolish stunts such as jumping over a cucumber frame. One of the boys might, in such an event, fail, and fall on the glass, with disastrous results. Some play this game with the rule that if a boy fails at anything the leader does, he at once goes out of the game. We here give a few stunts:

Climb a tree.

Turn a somersault.

Turn a Catherine-wheel.

Hop for ten yards on right leg, then change to left leg.

Run on all-fours.

Jump a flower-bed.

Run backwards.

Bunny jump.

Physical exercises.

Hop, holding other foot behind, then in front.

Hold little finger of the left hand with right hand, then put right foot through, then left, and bring arms up behind into an upright position without relinquishing hold of little finger. Now return by same stages to starting position.

Fold arms, lie down, and get up again without unfolding arms.

Jump a bush.

Of course, an umpire must be watching for failures.

Out and Home

In this game, first choose sides—as many as you please, so that the number of either side be equal. Next mark out a fairly large space as Home. Then toss for choice—that is, whether you will keep Home or go out to hide.

One side now goes out and hides; and when a signal is given, the Home side has to find them, and touch them before they reach Home. Leave two at Home to defend it, while the others go out to look for the enemy.

When once the signal is given, a boy need not wait for anyone to discover him, but should work his way round bushes, etc., and finally make a rush for Home. If he reaches this without being touched, it counts one to his side. If, however, he be touched, he retires as a prisoner, and it counts a point scored by the Home side. Whichever side secures the most points wins. Should one of the seekers discover a boy hiding behind a bush and cry out, "I spy Dick" (or "Harry," as the case may be), that player must at once dash for Home. Of course, the "spy" shouts in a loud voice, so that the two Home defenders may hear. They then at once know that a rush is being made for Home by someone; but while their attention is directed to that particular boy, others may choose this opportunity, and sprint for Home. If girls are playing, an equal number should be on either side, for boys usually run faster than girls. This may be described as one of the best of outdoor party games.

RELAY HOOP RACE

This game is usually played on a lawn. First mark out a fairly large circle. This may be done by placing articles on the ground (say, ten yards apart) to mark the course to be taken. A hoop (an iron one is best, of moderate size) will be needed, and two strong sticks with which to trundle it along. Let two boys, who will be captains, pick sides. It does not matter how many play, but the sides must be equal in number. Toss for choice of innings; then, when all is ready, the captain must say in what order the boys are to go.

No. 1 starts off as fast as he can with the hoop. He must keep on the outside of the articles on the ground, and race back to the starting post—when the next boy, with the second stick, must take his place, while the hoop is still trundling. He must go round in like manner as fast as possible, then pass the hoop on to boy No. 3, who has taken possession of the stick used by No. 1; and so on, until the team has been round. On no account must the hoop be touched by either hand, unless it fall, when it may be picked up and started again in exactly the same place. The race must be timed; and when all the boys on one side have been once round, the umpire must declare how long they have taken. Then the opposing team begins, and it is obvious that their object is to complete the rounds in less time than their opponents. The team with the shorter time naturally wins.

A great deal depends on how quickly one boy takes over the hoop from another. If this is done smartly, much time will be saved. The game may be played equally well by girls.

Hoop Obstacle Race

This is a pleasing variation of other races. First mark out any kind of course you think desirable, and then scatter various obstacles about same. For example, say ten yards from the start place two bricks about five inches apart, then three bricks (or any suitable substitute) in line about two yards from each other; ten yards farther on two more bricks five inches apart; then five yards beyond these a block of wood; and so on, to the end of the course.

On the opposite page we give a diagram which will suggest the track the hoop should take.

Each player now takes his turn. Those completing the course without mishap play off again, until one only is left in, who becomes the winner.

The first player starts with the hoop and stick, and has to go round or through all the obstacles successfully. Having started the hoop, he must touch it with nothing but the stick. Should the hoop fall to the ground or come in contact with any of the obstacles, he is out, and the next player then tries. Should it be found that several of the players have completed the course fairly easily, the umpire (who is chosen at the commencement of the game) must alter the position of the obstacles to make the task more difficult. He can, for instance, reduce the space between the bricks to four inches. This game is so fascinating that the grown-ups will be unable to resist its appeal.

START

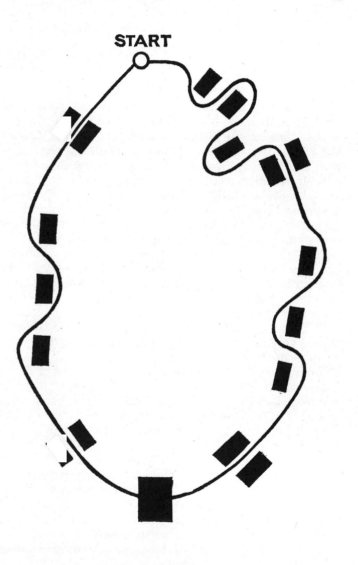

GAMES FOR A TEENAGE PARTY

SHOPPING EXPEDITION

THIS is a very noisy, robust game and care should be taken not to let it become out of hand. Appoint two people, one as story-teller and one as collector. Divide the rest of the guests into teams, five or six persons to a team is the ideal number. Each team now chooses one of their members to be a team leader. To play the game, the story-teller tells a little tale about a shopping expedition he, or she, recently undertook and in telling the story mentions several things that he either saw or bought. Each time one of these items is mentioned, the people in the game try to find a similar article which they give to their own team leader, who in turn takes it to the collector. The first team leader to present the object to the collector scores a point for his team. Thus, the story may go something like this:—

"The other day, I found that I had an odd pound (here everyone looks for a pound note to hand to their team leader) so I decided to enjoy myself with a shopping adventure. Taking a 'bus and paying for a fourpenny ticket (again, the search commences through pockets, handbags, etc., to find a fourpenny 'bus ticket), I went down into the High Street. In the first shop, I bought a ladies' handkerchief . . ." and so on until the story finishes.

Rules to remember, which must be strictly enforced, is that only team leaders may take the objects to the collector; objects must be *handed* to the collector, not thrown; time must be allowed after the mention of each item to allow all the team leaders to return to their teams; team leaders or members of teams may take any item mentioned from people in their own team, but on no account must they "raid" other teams

The story-teller should limit his "shopping list" to items likely to be in the possession of the players, but he can greatly add to the fun if, for instance, he claims to have bought an odd pair of shoes or two different coloured socks.

The collector should keep an accurate account of the points awarded to each team, and his verdict in the final analysis as to the winning team must be accepted.

WHO AM I?

Before the party prepare a number of slips of paper (allow two or three to each guest) on which the names of famous celebrities have been written—people such as Nelson, Wellington, Henry VIII, Cleopatra, Helen of Troy, Mary, Queen of Scots, and some modern stage, screen and television stars. As each guest arrives, pin one of these names on to his or her *back*, so that it cannot be seen by the person wearing it. The idea is for the guest to wander round the room and by a process of question and answer find out who they are. The questions asked must be put in such a way that only "Yes" or "No" may be given as an answer. For example, the guesser may ask "Am I a female", to which the answer can be given "Yes" or "No" as the case may be; but the player should not phrase his question "Am I a man or woman?".

This game is a great ice-breaker, particularly where some of the guests are not known to each other—it is very difficult to be shy with a beefy, rugger-type man who is trying to identify himself as Helen of Troy!

This is also a useful way of providing partners for everyone, and it can be arranged that suitable "personages" can be paired together—Henry VIII and Anne Boleyn; Romeo and Juliet; Anthony and Cleopatra, and so on.

News Item

Divide the guests into an equal number of girls and boys, seating the boys on one side facing the girls who are sitting about two chair-widths away. Give each boy a small newspaper cutting and each girl a pencil and piece of paper. The idea of the game is for the boy to dictate the news item to the girl sitting opposite him and for her to get it down with the minimum number of mistakes. As all the boys will be shouting out different news items at one time, this is not quite so easy as it sounds, and it requires quite a lot of concentration on the girls' part to listen only to their own partner and ignore the rest of the hubbub.

The first pair to get the message written down completely with not more than six mistakes are the winners.

Animal Zoo

This is another noisy game, greatly enjoyed by young people of all ages. Pair off the guests, boy to girl and tell each pair what their animal "call sign" is to be— "Moo" for a cow; "Miaow" for a cat and so on. Before the game commences have scattered around the rooms which are in use for the party small pieces of confetti or similar tokens. At the word "Go", each boy goes off to try to find a piece of paper, and when he has succeeded he picks it up and proceeds to call his partner by means of his own "call sign". His girl partner has then to try to locate him and when she finds him, he hands her the piece of paper and tries to find another piece and the same procedure is repeated. Obviously for this game, it is very necessary for several rooms, preferably upstairs and downstairs to be used, because if the girl can see her partner, she will not have to bother to listen for the "call sign".

After the girl has retrieved one of the tokens from her partner she must remain where she is until such time as she identifies his "call sign" once again; she must not attempt to follow him from room to room.

The couple with the largest number of tokens are the winners.

Messages

Let all the guests sit in one big circle. One of the players then turns to the player on his, or her, right and whispers a small simple message, perhaps something like "I see Mary is wearing a blue dress". The player who receives this message then whispers it to the next player on the right and so on right the way round the circle, until the whisper comes back to the originator. By this time, it bears little or no resemblance to the original message, and there is great merriment when the person who started the message tells the group what he said, and then what message was returned to him. The game can continue indefinitely, with a different person starting the whispering each time.

Indoor Hockey

For this game you need a soft woollen or cloth ball and two walking-sticks. Choose two teams of six a side and sit them on chairs facing each other with about four yards between each team. Place two other chairs at either end, in the centre of the space between the teams; these are the goal-posts, and appoint one goal-post to each team. Give each member of the team a number, one to six, numbering one team from left to right, and the other from right to left, so that both number ones are at opposite ends of the two rows. One person is appointed umpire and he, or she, throws the ball into the very centre of the space between the rows, and at the same time calling a number—say, "three". At this, both number threes leave their seats, pick up the walking-stick (which is always returned to number one after each "try"), run to the centre and with the crook of the stick, try to hit the ball into the opposing goal. The player managing to get the ball under the chair goal-post belonging to the other team, scores a "goal" for his side. When this has been achieved both players return the stick to their number one and resume their own places in the team. The game then continues, the umpire throwing the ball and calling numbers as before.

BLINDFOLD OBSTACLE RACE

First of all prepare the course. In a large room place a number of "obstacles" around the room—chairs, tables, forms, or any similar article of furniture can be used. Get the competitors to join in pairs and tie the inside legs of each couple together (as for the conventional three-legged race). Let the competitors have a good look at the course, and then blindfold them. Now turn the pairs round and round, so that they are not sure quite where they are facing. While this is being done, arrange for a confederate to remove all the obstacles very quietly, so that the main part of the room is clear. Then tell the players they may start the race. This is most amusing to watch as the blindfolded pairs will try most carefully to avoid the "obstacles" which the audience knows full well are not there.

WHAT'S THE SMELL?

Before the party, prepare a number of small muslin bags which contain various pungent smelling goods— e.g. coffee, lavender, curry powder, sage, lemon, thyme and so on—and put them on a tray. Ask each guest to smell each little bag and write down what they think it contains. It will be found that after the first two have been identified fairly easily, the sense of smell will become numb and it will be exceedingly difficult to identify the remainder. Give a small prize to the competitor who correctly names the highest number of "smells".

MYSTERY PARCEL

Have this prepared in advance. Put a small prize into a box, wrap it up in brown paper, and tie it round with string. Wrap this parcel, in its turn, in paper, and secure it with string. Continue in this manner until you have a very large parcel.

To play the game, have the guests sit round in a circle and arrange for someone to play the piano, or have a long playing record. The idea is for the parcel to be passed from person to person, so long as the music is playing, but as soon as it stops, the person holding the parcel must *untie* the string (do not make the knots too difficult), and remove the paper without tearing it. When the music starts again, the parcel must be immediately handed on as before. The last person opening the box which contains the prize, keeps their trophy.

ACT THE WORD

Let one player leave the room, while the others who are left behind choose an "acting" word, such as "coyly", "angrily", "scornfully", "happily" and so on. The player from outside then comes in and asks any of the others to do some action in "the manner of the word". For instance, he may ask someone to hand him a book in "the manner of the word". The person must then comply—supposing the word to be angrily, he will hand a book to the guesser in an angry fashion. The guesser continues to make similar requests of the other persons in the room until such time as he has guessed the word. The person whose action has given him the answer is then asked to leave the room, while another word is chosen.

PASSING THE BALL

For this you will need two tennis balls, or similar size playing balls. Seat the guests in two teams facing each other, so that they can sit with their legs outstretched without touching any member of the other team. Now place a ball on the ankles of each of the first members of the two teams. The object now is for each player to pass the ball on to the outstretched ankles of the next player, without dropping the ball on the floor. This may be achieved by turning the legs slightly sideways and gently dropping the ball on to the next players' ankles, or by holding the legs immediately over those of the next competitor and opening the ankles slowly and carefully and letting the ball drop gently through. If the ball falls on to the floor, it must be returned to the first player in the team, and the game started again. The team who first manages to pass the ball from end to end without dropping it are the winners.

BURSTING THE BALLOON

Ask for five or six "volunteers". Give each one of them a glass of water, a dry cracker biscuit and a balloon. The idea of the game is that the player must drink the glass of water, eat the biscuit and then blow up the balloon until it bursts. The first person to achieve this is the winner. This is more difficult than it sounds, since the act of drinking and eating, make the player feel very "full" and they find it very difficult.

BALLOON RELAY RACE

This game needs twelve players, six newspapers and six inflated balloons. The players form pairs and face each other at opposite ends of the room. The idea is for the players at one end to "flap" the balloon along the floor, by flapping the newspaper up and down to cause a draught, until it reaches his partner at the other end. The other player then takes the newspaper and "flaps" the balloon back to the starting point. The pair first completing the course are winners. This takes a certain amount of knack, as the flapping causes the balloon to drift in almost any direction except the one intended.

THE MYSTERY OF NUMBERS

THE study of numbers is a most fascinating subject, and although perhaps not suitable for very young people, those who are old enough to understand arithmetic will take great interest in the following surprising results, some of which will require a good deal of solving.

THE MAGIC NINE

Let us take the figure 9. Multiply it by any other number and add the digits of the product together. It will then be found that the unit value of the sum will be always nine.

Thus:

9×9 produces 81, equal to 8 and 1, or 9
9×8 ,, 72, ,, 7 ,, 2, ,, 9
9×7 ,, 63, ,, 6 ,, 3, ,, 9
9×6 ,, 54, ,, 5 ,, 4, ,, 9
9×5 ,, 45, ,, 4 ,, 5, ,, 9
9×4 ,, 36, ,, 3 ,, 6, ,, 9
9×3 ,, 27, ,, 2 ,, 7, ,, 9
9×2 ,, 18, ,, 1 ,, 8, ,, 9

In the series of figures 9 8 7 6 5 4 3 2 1 0, if we add together the first and last, second and eighth, third and seventh, we get the same effect, thus:

9 and 0 give 9, 8 and 1 give 9, 7 and 2 give 9, 6 and 3 give 9, 5 and 4 give 9. Also, if we add the figures from 0 to 9 together, we get the sum of 45, which again make 9.

THE LIGHTNING CALCULATOR

Here is an ingenious way of finding the sum of three rows of figures upon the first line being shown:

Ask anyone to set down a row of figures from left to right. It does not matter how many, but the effect is improved by limiting it to four figures, as, for example, 1,426.

Immediately these figures are written you may know that the sum of the figures (including 1,426) which are to be written will amount to 11,425. This is obtained by deducting 1 from the right-hand figure and placing it in front of the left-hand figure, so that the 6 becomes a 5, and the 1 becomes 11, the figures 42 remaining unchanged. Write the total 11,425 on a separate piece of paper.

Now get another person to write a row of four figures underneath those already set down. He writes let us say, 2,452. You now write the third row yourself, and in doing so you make your figure and that immediately above it equal to 9. Thus:

Figures written down ...	1,426
	2,452
So you write	7,547

And the total will be ...   11,425, as predicted.

If we want to find the total of five rows of figures, we get the first line written down, then subtract 2 from the right hand and transfer it to the extreme left. The second row is written by another person. The third row you write yourself, making up the nines each time as already explained. The fourth row is contributed by another person, and the last row is written by yourself, again making up to the nines. The total will then be the same as that predicted by you. Thus, let the first row be 32,678; the total sum will be 232,676.

And the second row...   65,432

Your row will be   ...   34,567, making up with
line above it to nines.

Another writes   ...   23,546

You write   76,453

The total being   ...   232,676, exactly as predicted.

For the total of seven rows of figures you must deduct 3 from the right-hand figure of the first row and transfer it, as before, to the left of the row, and you must yourself write the third, fifth, and seventh rows so as to total with the line above to nines.

This may be extended indefinitely to any number of rows, but for every two rows of figures added to the first row you must deduct one more. Thus, for three rows you deduct 1 from the right and transfer to left. For five rows you deduct 2 and transfer as before. For seven rows you deduct 3 and transfer it. For nine rows you deduct 5 and transfer it. The number of rows must always be an odd number, but the number of figures in the row does not affect the result. For show purposes it is better not to exceed four figures to the row.

FINDING A NUMBER THOUGHT OF

Let anybody think of a figure, but without naming it. Tell him to multiply it by 3 and add 1 to the product. Now let the sum be multiplied by 3 again, and to the product add the number thought of.

Let the result be declared. Then, to know the figure thought of you merely take away the last figure, and the other, or others, will be the number thought of.

Thus:

Number thought of ...	...	7
Multiplied by 3	... ...	21
Add 1	... ...	22
Multiply by 3	... ...	66
Add number thought of	...	7
		—
		73

Rejecting the units, we have 7 left, which is the required figure. Now let us try a more difficult one:

Number thought of	...	17
Multiplied by 3	... ...	51
Add 1	... ...	52
Multiplied by 3	... ...	156
Add number thought of	...	17
		—
		173

Rejecting the units, we have 17 left, which was the number of which the person thought.

THE CENTURY PUZZLE

Arrange the figures 1 to 9 so that they will amount to 100 when added together. Very few persons will be able to do this without a good deal of experiment and thought. This is one way of doing it:

$$
\begin{array}{r}
15 \\
36 \\
47 \\
\hline
98 \\
2 \\
\hline
100
\end{array}
$$

And this is another: 32

57

—

89
6

4
1

—

100

Other ways of solving this problem are left to the ingenuity of the reader.

THE CUTE LAWYER

A lawyer was once left executor to a will in which he was instructed to divide the testator's horses among three persons in the following proportions—namely, half to A, one-third to B, and one-ninth to C. When the will was signed there were eighteen horses in the stables, but between the signing of the will and the death of the testator one of the horses died, so that only seventeen remained to be divided in the proportions provided for in the will, which could not be done. But the cute lawyer saw a way out of the difficulty, and one that satisfied everybody. He gave a horse out of his own stable, making the number of horses to eighteen, as originally, and then divided the horses according to the will, at the same time receiving his own horse back.

Of the eighteen horses—

A receives half, or	9
B receives a third	6
C receives a ninth	2
	—
	17
The lawyer's horse	1
	—
	18

A Really Wonderful Number

The number 37 is a magical number. It happens to be the number of years from 4 B.C. to A.D. 33, during which the Founder of Christianity ministered. If you multiply this number by any of the figures of the arithmetical progression of 3—*i.e.*, 3, 6, 9, 12, 15, 18, etc.—you will derive a product which is composed of a triple repetition of the same figure. Thus:

37	37	37	37	37	37	37	37	37
3	6	9	12	15	18	21	24	27
111	222	333	444	555	666	777	888	999

Arithmetical Puzzles

Write down the figures 1 to 9 and add them together. Thus 1 plus 2 plus 3 plus 4 plus 5 plus 6 plus 7 plus 8 plus 9 equals 45. From 45 take 50 and leave 15.

45 is XLV, from which take L (which is 50), and you have left XV.

Take 1 from 19 and leave 20.

19 is XIX, from which take I, and you get XX, or 20, left.

Add 5 and 6 together to make 9.

Take six matches and place them vertically on the table. Now take five matches and place them so that the first, laid diagonally, makes the letter N; the second, placed diagonally between the fourth and fifth uprights, makes another N; while the three remaining matches, placed horizontally against the last upright, will make the letter E. The figure when completed will spell NINE. So that by adding five matches to six matches you make the required number.

Place three sixes together so as to make seven.
Six and six-sixths, or $6\frac{6}{6}$

PECULIAR FIGURES

$$15{,}873 \times 7 \text{ equals } 111{,}111$$
$$31{,}746 \times 7 \text{ ,, } 222{,}222$$
$$47{,}619 \times 7 \text{ ,, } 333{,}333$$
$$63{,}492 \times 7 \text{ ,, } 444{,}444$$
$$79{,}365 \times 7 \text{ ,, } 555{,}555$$
$$95{,}238 \times 7 \text{ ,, } 666{,}666$$
$$111{,}111 \times 7 \text{ ,, } 777{,}777$$
$$126{,}984 \times 7 \text{ ,, } 888{,}888$$
$$142{,}857 \times 7 \text{ ,, } 999{,}999$$

The value for $\frac{1}{7}$ expressed in decimals is .142857

,,	,,	$\frac{2}{7}$	,,	,,	,,	.285714
,,	,,	$\frac{3}{7}$	,,	,,	,,	.428571
,,	,,	$\frac{4}{7}$	,,	,,	,,	.571428
,,	,,	$\frac{5}{7}$	,,	,,	,,	.714285
,,	,,	$\frac{6}{7}$	,,	,,	,,	.857142

while $\frac{7}{7}$, or 1, is only   .999999

The figures for each seventh are repeated in different order, and in every case the last figure of the series is the result of multiplying digit by 7. Thus $\frac{1}{7}$ gives 1×7, or 7, and the series is .142857, ending with 7. And $\frac{2}{7}$ is 2×7, or 14, the series being .285714, ending in 4. And this continues throughout the series, so that the correct order of the decimal may always be known. Thus:

1×7 is	7,	which is the last figure in	.142857
2×7 is	14,	and 4	,,	,,	,,	.285714
3×7 is	21,	,, 1	,,	,,	,,	.428571
4×7 is	28,	,, 8	,,	,,	,,	.571428
5×7 is	35,	,, 5	,,	,,	,,	.714285
6×7 is	42,	,, 2	,,	,,	,,	.857142
7×7 is	49,	,, 9	,,	,,	,,	.999999

MORE THOUGHT-READING

Ask a person to think of a number but not to mention it. Ask him to double it. Tell him to add any even number you yourself choose (taking care to remember what that number is). Next ask him to halve the whole, and then to take away the first number he thought of. The answer in each case will be half the number you told him to add.

Example:

Number thought of is   20
Double it is   ...   40
Add, say 10   ...   50
Half this is   25
Number thought of —20
————
Leaves   ...   5, which is half of the 10 added

To Discover a Person's Age

Let a person put down the number of the month in which he was born, thus: January 1, February 2, March 3, April 4, May 5, etc. Double this number. Add 5. Multiply by 50. Add age last birthday. Subtract 365. Add 115. He must then tell you the figures that are left as a result of the operation. If there are two figures, the last will be age and the first will be the month in which he was born. If there are three figures, the last two will be his age and the first will be the month. If there are four figures, the last two will be his age and the first two will be the month.

Example:

Born in July   ...   7th month
Multiply by 2 ...   14
Add 5   19
Multiply by 50...   950
Add age, 16   ...   966
Subtract 365   ...   601
Add 115   ...   716

Result: July (7), aged 16.